HOW CARNFORTH GREW

A
SIMPLE OUTLINE
TO 1900 A.D.

BY MARION RUSELL

Published by Lundarien Press, UK
Copyright © Marion Russell 1997

ISBN 978-1-910816-65-3

For more info and other books in this series:
www.lundarienpress.com

Other Books in the
'History of Carnforth' Series

2. How Carnforth Steamed into the 20th Century

3. A Childhood in Carnforth

CONTENTS

INTRODUCTION

When my husband, Jim, and I retired in 1980, looking up my paternal and maternal family trees became one of my pleasant pastimes.

My father, Thomas Wilkinson, was born in 'The Dolly-tub Row' in Cragbank, and my mother Annie Barnham came to live here when she was a little girl. Through them, I became interested in Carnforth's story and, during the last 15 years, I have enjoyed recording all the snippets about my hometown which I could find. As I am now in my 82nd year and time is running out, I decided to arrange all my information in chronological order and write a simple outline of how Carnforth grew, dedicating it to the memory of my parents and grandparents, who loved our town so much.

I have done my very best to make this a true record and, for any errors and omissions, I apologise to those who are better informed.

Marion Russell (nee Wilkinson)
Born in 1915
at 13 Hill Street
Carnforth

CARNFORTH

Situated in the North-West coastal tip of Lancashire, Carnforth is close to the borders of Cumbria, Yorkshire and the late-lamented Westmorland. Its position has an effect on its history and development.

EARLY SPELLING OF THE TOWN'S NAME:

CHRENEFORDE in the Doomsday Book.

KERNEFORDE in 1310.

CARNEFORTH in the 16th Century.

THE DERIVATION OF ITS NAME?

1) Crane's Ford - a crossing place on the river where cranes (herons) nested.

2) Cairn Ford - cairn, a pyramid of rough stones built as a memorial or landmark.

3) Kerne-Ford - a crossing place on the River Keer.

4) Kereforth - a estuary of the Keer.

THE KEER - CARNFORTH'S RIVER

Former spelling 'KERNE' and 'KERE'. It arises out of the moor on the edge of what was formerly Westermorland, and runs to KEREHOLM and DOCKER.

On its short course to the sea it used to turn mills

at BORWICK, CAPENWRAY and WARTON (Millhead).

Before entering MORECAMBE BAY at Carnforth, it is augmented by the wonderful MEERBECK subterranean brook from DUNNAL MILL, near Over Kellet, where spectacular caves could be entered.

IN THE BEGINNING

During the Ice Age a great glacier swept down towards what is now Carnforth and this frozen stream chipped and ground up all the rocks and stones in its course. This accounts for the valuable deposits of sand and gravel in the area.

The Romans

Almost 2000 years ago, the Romans found an arm of the sea running inland, near to the village of Borwick.

It entered between the eminences of WARTON CRAG and what is now HAGG FARM, and then widened and flowed over the levels inland, roughly following the course of the RIVER KEER.

View of Warton Crag from the top of Netherbeck Hill - Upper North Road (formerly Old Coach Road). In Roman times, the valley below was under water when an arm of the sea reached as far as Dock Acres near Borwick.

The present Burton road dips into and passes through the former bed of the bay. "Old Carnforth" was eventually built on the higher ground above sea level.

Near the head of the inlet, the ROMANS constructed extensive dockage at the point still known as DOCK ACRES.

The remains of very old vessels were excavated here, and a local blacksmith got possession of an ancient anchor.

Some Roman soldiers may have been transferred by sea from the camp at LANCASTER to HADRIAN'S WALL. Perhaps they sailed up CARNFORTH BAY to take on board provisions by trading ... or pillaging.

The Roman Legions left Britain in 406 AD.

SAXON TIME (from 600 AD)

It is to JOHN LUCAS, a local historian born in the late 17th century that we owe much of our knowledge of Carnforth in ancient times.

He was born in "Carnford", educated in Warton at the school founded by Archbishop Hutton, and was brought up in Leeds where he became a schoolmaster.

Between the years 1710 and 1755, he compiled an extensive description of Warton Parish, which included Carnforth, and told of its history, its inhabitants and also about the local flora and fauna.

His work remained in manuscript form.

GALLIHAW FARM

(later spelling Galley Hall Farm)

This building stands on an eminence near Carnforth shore.

Lucas wrote that our Saxon ancestors gave the name 'Gallihaw' to this little hill because, at its foot, there had once been a haven for galleys. A change of river-course had, at one time, washed away acres of land, and a quantity of ships' timbers had been found nearby.

This could have been the place where Saxons first invaded the area before eventually settling here.

Galley Hall Farm (as today)
Built on the side of GALLIHAW, a small ancient port where ships were built till the late 1600s.

MOOTHAW

A hillock in the Netherbeck area was where OLD SAXON COURTS were said to be held. A 'FOLK-MOOT' was a public assembly where quarrels were settled, local problems discussed and crime punished. An accused man sometimes had to prove his innocence by ordeal, e.g. by water, fire or combat. In the case of water, he might be thrown into a deep pond. If he floated, he was declared guilty. If he sank he was innocent (but drowned!).

The ancient courts wielded a strong deterrent for nagging wives. They could be made to wear a SCOLD'S BRIDLE, which had a piece of iron to go into the mouth and hold down the tongue. No Carnforth wife would want to be seen wearing one of those!

Written laws and trial by jury were not introduced until the reign of King Henry II (1154-1189). *[The old English word Mōt gave us our word for 'meeting', and we still speak of a Moot point.]*

COTE STONES

This place lies on the River Keer at the head of the sands and is probably so named from the stones that lie on the shore.

The River Keer
Photographed from Shore Road before it enters the waters of Morecambe Bay.

John Lucas wrote that tradition confidently affirmed that THE DANES landed here, in order to rob and pillage, in the year 966 when Thoredus, the son of Gunnar, laid waste this part of Lancashire.

Originally, Carnforth was part of the Parish of BOLTON IN SABULUM (i.e. Bolton on the Sands).

14

Then, in the year 1208, it was transferred to WARTON PARISH for over 650 years.

THE MIDDLE AGES

GILBERT, who died in 1170, was BARON OF KENDAL and LORD OF WARTON.

His descendants, who added DE LANCASTER to their names, built castles at KENDAL and MOURHOLME.

Around the year 1300, MOURHOLME CASTLE was a large imposing building (probably built of stone), which stood on a gravel mound above marshes in the lower KEER VALLEY. It dominated the whole area.

The site of Mourholme was positively identified in 1975 but its massive foundations were lost because of gravel extraction at Dock Acres quarry.

Medieval pottery and a diamond ring were recovered before all traces of the castle were destroyed. *[PINE LAKE now covers a large part of this area.]*

Gilbert's family dominated the district until the early 14 hundreds.

[In very broad simple terms: Medieval villages, such as Warton, were organised as MANORS. The TENANTS paid rent and did various services for the LORD.

THE LORD OF WARTON who was also LORD OF CARNFORTH, was himself a tenant of the LORD OF LANCASTER and he was in turn a tenant of the King.

A lord who held a large and important group of manors was known as a BARON & his estates together were called a BARONY.]

An Ancient Hostelry 1620
The CARNFORTH INN before modernisation. Photographed around 1880. Note the absence of the church tower and the Country Hotel.

1620 - THE CARNFORTH INN

In this year, the town's oldest public building was erected..

This ANCIENT HOSTELRY was a simple, rectangular building until it was extensively enlarged and modernised in 1904.

1638 - HAGG FARM

This is Carnforth's oldest house, and belonged to JAMES AND ALICE LUCAS. Their initials are carved in stone over the door, and they were relatives of John Lucas. He recorded that the Saxons called a mansion-house 'HAGA' and used the word 'Hag' for a hedge. He thought it possible that a mansion had stood on this site for over 900 years.

Hagg Farm - 1638

Carnforth's oldest house. Home of James and Alice Lucas, relatives of John Lucas, the local historian born at Brigg End, his nearby home.

AUG 1650 - KING CHARLES II

With 14,000 Royalist troops, Charles halted for a day and camped locally on high ground in a field called BARTHERHOLME, a meadow covering 12-14 acres, which frequently flooded. It is in the Netherbeck area.

Charles, who had been crowned in Scotland after his father CHARLES I had been beheaded, was on his way south to claim the throne. Whilst in this vicinity, he journeyed on about half a mile to BORWICK HALL, where he was regaled by Sir Richard Bindloss.

He and his army did not reach London. They were defeated at the BATTLE OF WORCESTER in 1651 by OLIVER CROMWELL, Lord Protector of the Commonwealth ... but Charles escaped.

1660 - HEARTH TAX

People at this time were taxed according to the number of hearths in their homes.

Carnforth's returns read as follows:

1) 1 house (Richard Mason's) had 4 hearths.

2) 1 house (Robert Dawson's) had 3 hearths.

3) 8 houses had 2 fires each.

4) 23 houses had 1 fire each.

Thus Carnforth's 33 homes paid tax for 46 hearths. From this information it could be assumed that Carnforth's population at this time was approximately 100-150.

Over the years, various taxes were levied, e.g. SHIP TAX, TEA TAX, CARRIAGE TAX and WINDOW TAX. The Vikings even put a tax on Breathing! If you didn't pay up, your nostrils were slit or your nose was cut off.

NOTABLE EVENTS IN BRITISH HISTORY

1665 - The Great Plague.

1666 - The Great Fire of London.

1668 - The building of Carnforth's 2nd Oldest House - a farm with an adjacent barn. *[On the site of its orchard the COUNCIL SCHOOL was built.]*

10 Lower North Road
Carnforth's second-oldest house, 1688

1676 - AN EARLY ROAD

Part of a set of playing cards first showed a road from WARRINGTON to KENDAL (they were taken from JOHN OGILBY'S great survey of main highways of Britain, published in the form of a series of ship maps). They show the main road leaving Bolton-le-Sands, arriving at Carnforth and then leaving along North Road.

LATTER HALF OF THE 1600S

DICK O'WILLS CLOSE - this was a field east of GALLIHAW.

John Lucas wrote that his father knew the DICK

referred to. He was a constable of the 'town' and was the last of a family here which had retained the ancient British way of using only Christian names followed by the place of abode of their forbears.

The use of surnames had become established from personal choice, e.g.:

5) <u>Occupation</u>: Butcher, Baker, Farmer, Smith, Cook.

6) <u>Place of Abode</u>: Woods, Lane, Hill, Forest, Rivers.

7) <u>Hair Colour</u>: Black, Grey, White, Black.

8) <u>Appearance and Characteristics</u>: Long, Short, Smart, Quick, Sharp, Beard, Cross, Good, Proudlove, Shufflebottom, etc. etc. etc.

LUCAS'S EARLY MEMORIES OF GALLIHAW

"This place was anciently noted for the building of merchant ships … and, up until now, 'The CONTENT' was built when I was a schoolboy … It is at present visited by 'barks and pinks' from Scotland, Ireland, the Isle of Man and the western coasts of England." Later he wrote, "It is now almost quite forsaken by sea-faring men."

HOMES

Lucas recorded that, in his lifetime, the town consisted of about 40 families. The houses, mostly thatched, stood at a considerable distance from each other. Some were unlofted and one was without a chimney. They were all built near water - river, stream, spring or well. Several humble cottages were built of hazel wattlings, daubed with mortar made of loam and straw and "overdrawn with a thin plaister of lime." Rushes were spread on the floor.

Lucas wrote, "A beggar belonging to this town is as rare as a horse in the streets of Venice."

WELLS

The locality of the following wells was noted: THROSTLETHWAITE WELL, BUTTERWELL, POLECAT WELL, STANK WELL, HOLY WELL.

Wells were of importance, not just as a source of drinking water, but because they were reputed to cure such complaints as scurvy and sore eyes etc. Words such as HAGS, THWAITES, GRUBBENS, WOODS and COPPICES affirm that Carnforth had anciently been woodland but, in later days, it was in danger of becoming almost treeless.

Most surrounding settlements had a church and a village green. Carnforth, having neither, remained a hamlet for many years.

Too much land was enclosed and owned by absent landlords.

The inhabitants would have benefited from more commonland, but would have needed more compost and hands to till the soil.

Over the years, Carnforth had been given away as a bequest, a dowry and a gift.

The many fields had to be given names so that tithes could be levied and paid at the Tithe Barn.

FIELD NAMES (OR AREAS)

[Some are still familiar to old Carnforthians]

Sleeping Dub, Elfa, Toad Plud, Ora, Salter Flat, Cow Close, Crae Pits, Potters Park, The Oven, Whinney Close, Batherholme, Orchard, Hall Gowins, Hall Croft, Thwaite, Huthwaite, The Banks, Robin Cross, Long Haws.

(Several of the latter were eventually used to name streets or houses, e.g. Bank Terrace, Hewthwaite Terrace, Haws Hill, Robin Hill and Hall Gowan.)

Mr Jonathan Peel, who owned COW CLOSE, did not put oxen to work pulling ploughs until they were three years old. (Oxen did not pull wains - wagons - in this parish.) Because the ground was stony, the oxen had to be shod. They had 2 little iron plates nailed to each foot.

HARVEST TIME

A hired fiddler went from field to field playing tunes for the tired reapers, whose backs were bent from their toil in the hot sun.

After a few brisk dances, their muscles were relaxed so that they could return to their labour with redoubled vigour and energy.

HARVEST FESTIVAL

Each family contributed malt, which was brewed into ale for the whole village. After supper, old people smoked their pipes with pleasure and delight, whilst young people spent their evening singing and dancing.

MARSH LAND

Towards the shore were inner and outer marshes, separated by a bank, called 'The Strand', which held back the salt water.

Lucas wrote that, in his time, marshland was of great service to the people. It provided:

1. Rich food and physic for cattle.

2. Turf for fuel.

3. Sods for roofing and for garden walls.

4. Seaweed for manure.

5. Rushes for parlour floors. (Rush-bearing was an annual festival in many villages.)

[Today local marshes are kept as sanctuaries for water fowl.]

ANCIENT IRONWORKS

It is surmised that, away back in time, Carnforth had some ancient ironworks. On a mound which was once an islet in 'Carnforth Bay', traces of old furnaces were once discovered.

THE OLD SHREW TREE

(Probably in the Netherbeck area.)

A certain old willow tree featured in local folklore. Farmers believed that shrews bit their animals and caused them sickness, so they caught as many as possible. Having pushed the unfortunate wee creatures into a hole in the tree's trunk, they blocked up the entrance.

This cruel practice was believed to give the twigs magical powers, when plucked off by the tree's owner. Folk had faith that their sick animals would be cured when touched with one of the wonderful wands.

Lucas wrote, "the noted SHREW TREE, till a few years ago, was almost superstitiously resorted to, but nowadays people begin to see the vanity of these charm-like remedies."

It seems that nowadays people once again have faith in strange superstitions. They believe that carrying a 4-leaf clover or a rabbit's foot can bring good fortune. On the other hand, bad luck will follow if they walk under ladders, put up umbrellas indoors, wear green garments, cross knives etc.

Star signs in newspapers are avidly read, fortune-tellers are consulted (even those who sit under blue plastic pyramids!) and strange rituals are followed before lottery numbers are chosen.

Belief in the old Shrew Tree's magical powers was perhaps not as foolish as was first imagined!

[The ancient Shrew Tree may still exist. The advent of new roads, the canal and the railway have made the directions given by Lucas difficult to follow.]

POTTERS' PARK

A fine sort of blue clay, which the inhabitants called 'POTTERS' CLAY, was to be found in an area by the banks of the Keer.

[Gardeners watch out for pieces of blue pottery which you may dig up!]

SALT COTES

On the edge of the sands, west of GALLIHAW, is SALT COTES, so named because there once stood there little houses for the making of salt. Lucas gives a long description of how a grey type of salt was produced here.

STAGECOACH DAYS

In the early days, before Macadam and Telford introduced good methods of road-building, travelling could be very uncomfortable and dangerous.

Parishes only took care of the roads near their villages, so long stretches of the highways were neglected and they didn't always connect up with each other. Guides were sometimes necessary. Any farmer ploughing up parts of the highway could be prosecuted.

The journey from LONDON to EDINBURGH took 10 days in summer and 12 days in winter. Summer brought clouds of dust and, in winter, it was known for stagecoaches to disappear into very deep, rain-filled ruts.

To raise money for the upkeep of roads, toll-gates were built at which travellers were made to pay towards the cost of repairs. To prevent riders and drivers from dashing past without paying, a law was made that roads could be blocked by a turn-pike, a gate with spikes.

[I remember the local toll-gate building which stood near KEER VILLAS at the start of the road to Silverdale. It was demolished in my youth.]

The lonely road between Capernwray and Over Kellet was said to be the haunt of lawless HIGHWAYMEN. True, perhaps. On the other hand, it could have been a rumour to add a little excitement to rural life in Carnforth.

EARLY 1700s

THE JOURNEY NORTHWARD (AROUND 1700 AD)

[This is purely supposition on my part. Before trying to picture the route of very old roads, it is necessary to eliminate the railway, the canal, modern roads and all buildings less than 300 years old]

The Low Road?
Stage coaches used the High Road N-S
Note the big upright stones which may have marked the side of the Low Road, used by people on foot or horse-back. It crosses the Spring Field and skirts Bolton Brow.

Before proceeding northward, did travellers have a choice of 2 routes on reaching the Cross Hill area of BOLTON LE SANDS?

Was route (1) THE HIGH ROAD, which was the best for wheeled vehicles because it was on firm ground away from marshes and land liable to be flooded?

This route would go to NETHER KELLETT, on to The Green at OVER KELLET, turn down the hill to CARNFORTH, go up the OLD COACH ROAD, down the steep hill to NETHERBECK and eventually head for BURTON, a busy centre for stagecoaches.

Was route (2) THE LOW ROAD, more convenient for travellers on foot or horseback?

This route would head directly to what is the Cragbank district of Carnforth now. It would skirt BOLTON BROW and keep to land high enough to be safe from marshes and areas which are quite often flooded by the tide.

At some period, THE TRAVELLERS' REST was built at the roadside to welcome tired people.

[In the census of 1881, the innkeeper was William Sarginson.]

OLD CARNFORTH

NORTH ROAD is still referred to as OLD CARNFORTH by its senior citizens.

When stagecoaches, pulled by 2 or 4 horses, became a popular means of transport, this area was the busiest in Carnforth. Houses, farms and cottages were built at each side of THE OLD COACH ROAD (It was not called NORTH ROAD until after the census of 1881.)

Ostlers cared for tired horses at a STAGING POST, which was built on the site of what was SLINGER'S

FARM in my young days. *[Today it is a private house next door to MERESBECK RESIDENTIAL HOME.]*

Passengers, who were also weary after long, uncomfortable journeys, could find refreshment and accommodation at THE GOLDEN BALL INN (demolished) and, in later days, at THE SHOVEL INN (built in 1750).

STANK WELL

Lucas wrote that, beside the old high road, there was a well, surrounded by a stone kerb on which was written "GARSTANG - HERRINGSYKE". He supposed it was supplied from a pool, known as HARE TARN lying a short distance to the east. The name STANK WELL could be a corruption of STANKELD (The Old English word 'STANG' meant a pool), because it was like a pool not a spring on stony ground.

(The census of 1881 stated that James Morrison lived at STANKELL HOUSE, Old Coach Road.

Today, behind Carnforth House in Upper North Road, a well has recently had a kerb built around it and a grill placed on top for safety.)

CARNFORTH'S FIRST PLACE OF WORSHIP

Because Carnforth did not have a place of worship before 1703, people had to walk to WARTON or OVER KELLET to attend church services, unless they owned a horse and could ride or drive there.

The Old Presbyterian Chapel 1703
Originally behind the GOLDEN BALL INN (demolished) on the Old Coach Road. Now concealed by these two doors at the back of the Shovel Inn.

For both young and old, those long walks would be very arduous, especially in bad weather.

This must have been a matter of concern for WARTON'S PRESBYTERIANS because they decided to open a chapel close to the OLD COACH ROAD. It was licensed for worship in 1703, and the people of Carnforth seemed to welcome its opening. Around 1720, it had a congregation of 138.

Unfortunately, the cause declined eventually and the township authorities took possession of the building. At one time, it became A SCHOOL and, from 1849, the WESLEYAN METHODISTS used it until a new chapel was opened on Lancaster Road in 1870.

[There are 2 dwellings nearby which were named as OLD CHAPEL HOUSE and OLD CHAPEL COTTAGE in the census of 1881. Today, they are known as LABURNUM HOUSE and LABURNUM COTTAGE. The owner of one of them says that, according to the deeds of her home, it is still part of the Parish of Warton.

The old chapel building, behind the SHOVEL INN, is concealed by modern cement facing and 2 brightly painted garage doors.

I remember that there was once a blacksmith's smithy behind the right-hand-side door.]

HUTHWAITE

In the Western part of the township, anciently woodland, were 5 large common fields. One was named THWAITE and the other four, contiguous to each other, were called HUTHWAITES (Hugh's Thwaites?)

A fine sand, suitable for scouring pewter, was dug from a sand-hill near the roadside on land adjoining Huthwaite. *[During my childhood it was an old sand-and-gravel hole. Today it is an industrial site.]*

Lucas wrote that, by the roadside near the sand hill, was a hollow place called THE FOUL FLUSH which sometimes overflowed so that the road was scarce passable.

[This problem still remains after 300 years!

Whenever there is a heavy downpour, the dip in the road at the foot of Hewthwaite Terrace becomes flooded and there is a traffic holdup.

The houses which make up Hewthwaite Terrace are now uninterestingly known as numbers 102-146 Lancaster Road.]

LONG HAWS

Also in the western area of Carnforth, there was some high ground called THE HAAS or HAWS, (an ancient word for hills). The land on these hills was sandy gravel with a thin coating of soil.

There was a level place on the HAWS near the meeting place of 2 highways (one probably going in the direction of the Carnforth Inn & northwards and the other heading towards Warton down what is now Haws Hill).

Each MIDSUMMER DAY village children assembled on this flat area to make bonfires called ST JOHN'S FIRES, and then diverted themselves by running around them or jumping over them. John Lucas recalled that he once helped to drag the skeleton of a horse over half a mile to build up a bonfire.

SAINT JOHN THE BAPTIST was remembered, too, on Midsummer Eve, when lighted torches were carried in his honour.

THE HAWS must have been a favourite meeting place for children, because it was there that they used to play handball in the Easter Holy Days. This was before a tithe barn was built on one part of the level area and another part was made an "intake".

ANOTHER ROYAL VISITOR

Was there great excitement in Carnforth in 1745? Did most of the inhabitants (still only 100-150) rush out to see BONNIE PRINCE CHARLIE, the Young Pretender, arrive with his army, kilts swinging on the march from Scotland to claim the English throne from King George II.

Both Prince Charlie and King George were descendants of King James VI of Scotland, who became King James l of England.

The troops are reputed to have halted in the LONG HAWS area, because some relics from this 2ND JACOBITE REBELLION were excavated from TUERS GRAVEL PIT and sent to the British Museum. In later years, the pit was known as HAWS HILL GRAVEL HOLE.

The Mannex Directory of 1881 stated that human bones, skulls and even skeletons were found only 2 feet below the soil's surface in the gravel hole. These would have had no connection with Bonnie Prince Charlie's visit, however.

[When I was a child, the site had ceased to be worked, and its lunar-like landscape was taken over by hen runs, pig sties and huts for various purposes.

Haws avenue estate now occupies this area.]

And Bonnie Prince Charlie's rebel army? It got no further than Derby.

TOAD PLUD

In the area at the foot of LONG HAWS was a pool or pond of standing water. It was given the name TOAD PLUD because of the amphibians which abounded there.

KRAE PITS

This was a little moss between TOAD PLUD and HALL YATE (GATE), which had retained its Saxon name, KRAE meaning crow.

Lucas wrote that when traditionally CARNFORTH HALL had stood on rising ground nearby, huntsmen kept horse-flesh for dogs in pits, and that caused the place to be haunted by crows.

(In the census of 1881 there was mention of a later CARNFORTH HALL, which was situated in what became Market Street.)

THE COMING OF GREAT CHANGES

Carnforth remained a small rural hamlet for many years with just a few additional farms, cottages or houses, mostly alongside the Old Coach Road. In the year 1801, the population numbered 219. (Bolton-le-Sands at that time had 639 inhabitants). 50 years later, in 1851, the number had only risen to 294.

This was still the AGE OF THE HORSE. Horses

worked for the farmers. People travelling distances rode on stagecoaches. Families who could afford it owned their own carriages, pony-traps, etc. Others used "SHANK'S PONY".

Goods were transported at a speed of between 2 and 3mph in huge covered stage-wagons - heavy, wide-wheeled vehicles, pulled by teams of 8 to 10 horses. Around 30 to 40 poor people could pay to huddle together on bales of merchandise as passengers.

Strings of pack-horses, laden with bundles of goods, were used on ground unsuitable for vehicles with wheels.

NOW GREAT CHANGES LAY JUST AHEAD!

THE INDUSTRIAL REVOLUTION

Between 1750 and 1839 in England, THE INDUSTRIAL REVOLUTION was taking place. THIS WAS THE GREAT DIVIDING LINE IN HUMAN DEVELOPMENT.

Ways had to be found to move people and heavy bulky goods quickly and efficiently. JAMES WATT had invented the STEAM ENGINE and GEORGE STEPHENSON the LOCOMOTIVE ENGINE: The Rocket.

The spinning and weaving of cloth changed from being cottage industries and moved into large factories, built to accommodate the clever textile machines invented by JAMES HARGREAVES, RICHARD ARKWRIGHT, RICHARD CROMPTON etc.

There was a need for a great deal of coal to be mined. Blast furnaces had to be built for the production of iron-ore. Sand, gravel and stones were necessary for the construction of good roads and railways.

CARNFORTH WAS READY AND WAITING FOR PROGRESS.

The first step forward was the building of the canal, which was proposed to connect WESTHOUGHTON with KENDAL.

Canals had become fashionable with the opening, in 1776, of the Bridgewater Canal between

Manchester and Liverpool. They became known as LIQUID ROADS and speeded transport, because a horse can pull a one-ton load on land but can move 20 tons on water.

Preston - Kendal Canal
Digging started at TEWITFIELD near Carnforth in 1792.
This is the Carnforth end of the Hincaster Tunnel.
There is no towpath

Second image is looking through the brick-lined, 378 yard long Hincaster tunnel.
There was a rope along the side for bargees to pull, or they could lie on their backs and 'walk' the barge along.

Early in 1792, the contractors, PINKERTON AND MURRAY, were given the go-ahead to start building a stretch of the canal from Carnforth's TEWITFIELD to ELLEL GREEN - a task which took

5 years to complete the 17 miles. The problem was the aqueduct over the River Lune at Lancaster.

Diggers (cutters) trudged tens and even hundreds of miles to become canal-workers. These navigators (navvies) lived nomadic lives. They earned 2s 2d a day for their labours. Stone masons who built the bridges were better paid, 3s 0d daily. Three bridges were built in Carnforth:

1) VICARAGE BRIDGE (in the Welmar district now).

2) KELLET ROAD BRIDGE.

3) THWAITE BRIDGE (Cragbank area).

In 1797, the PRESTON-TEWITFIELD length was completed. It was 41.5 miles long.

Horse-drawn barges could then sail to CARNFORTH laden with coal from the SOUTH LANCASHIRE COALFIELD. A basin had been made in the Hewthwaite area and this enabled the boats to be turned round ready for the return trip to Preston, carrying loads of stones, sand and gravel of which Carnforth had an abundance (thanks to that Ice Age glacier!)

The locality began to look as though a giant was taking huge bites out of the countryside as gravel holes were dug all around.

The last 15 miles of the canal, from TEWITFIELD to KENDAL, were not opened until 1819, hills having caused problems. The land from Tewitfield to HINCASTER rises 60 feet, so a 'flight' of 8 LOCKS had to be built. *[A canal cottage was built at the top, and a great uncle of mine, Mr Shuttleworth, was the lock keeper and bank ranger there at one time.]*

A reservoir at KILLINGTON and a tunnel through a hill, about 5 miles south of Kendal, entailed 2 more major engineering works. HINCASTER TUNNEL was 378 yards long and, after rock and earth had been removed, bricklayers took on the task of lining it with bricks. Unfortunately a towpath was not made, so horses had to be unharnessed and led up part of the hill. After going through a short tunnel, they were led down to the canal to meet up with the barge again. The boatmen had propelled their vessel through the darkness by pulling on a rope which ran along the inside of the tunnel.

A grand opening was organised at Kendal to celebrate the completion of the canal's 57 miles length. Busy barges sailed southward laden with limestone, timber, sand and gravel and made the return journey from Preston carrying loads of coal.

When PACKET BOATS for passengers were introduced in 1820, a time-table read as follows:

1) KENDAL - 6AM

2) TEWITFIELD - 9AM

3) LANCASTER - 1AM

4) GARSTANG - 4PM

5) PRESTON - 8PM.

14 hours! Today it could be done in less than one hour by car.

Fares for passengers were 4 shillings (20p) for 2nd class accommodation, and 6 shillings (30p) for 1st class.

The boats were heated in winter and refreshments could be obtained onboard or at a packet-boat inn alongside the canal (e.g. THE PACKET BOAT INN, Bolton-le-Sands).

A bank-ranger's cottage (now unoccupied) was built by the basin here, and alongside it were stables where the barge horses could be fed and rested whilst coal was being unloaded at the busy yard close by. (The site is now occupied by the BP GARAGE.)

In 1833, EXPRESS PACKET BOATS were used to try and cut down the travelling time from 14 hrs to 7 hours by using 4 galloping horses. They were not a success because their speed was detrimental to the canal banks.

By this time however, the DAY OF THE CANAL had begun to fade. A new and quicker form of transport was beginning to take over...

THE RAILWAY

The CANAL AGE had not added to Carnforth's population in any noticeable way, but the coming of the railway would eventually lead to sweeping changes.

In 1820, the PRESTON TO LANCASTER JUNCTION RAILWAY was opened with the northern terminus at Greaves Station (upper Penny Street, Lancaster).

Travellers now wishing to come to Carnforth had a choice of transport from Preston and places south. They could:

1) Travel all the way by stage-coach.

2) Ride on the Junction Railway to Lancaster and then transfer to a packet boat.

3) Sail all the way.

Passengers to Kendal had the same choices, but the locks beyond Carnforth were very inconvenient. Sometimes people saved time by disembarking at Tewitfield and walking up the towpath with their luggage to another boat, waiting at the top of the locks.

There was keen rivalry for passengers between the canal and the railway companies. Fares were cut as an enticement. At one time, the canal company owned the railway, but it was inevitable that, in the race for supremacy, the speedier railway would be the winner.

In 1844, work was started to extend the Junction Railway to Carlisle. The imposing new CASTLE STATION was built at Lancaster. The old Greaves Station continued to be used for many years but only for goods traffic.

Carnforth was proud to acquire a small HALT on the new PRESTON TO CARLISLE RAILWAY. It consisted of one platform, 30 feet long, which had no shade except a wooden porch, and was run by a staff of ONE *[that is ONE more than it has now!]* It was not on the site of our present station but a short distance north-east.

QUEEN VICTORIA was crowned in 1837. The 295 people of Carnforth doubtless celebrated the auspicious occasion in some appropriate rural ways.

FIVE LITTLE CAVES

In the SPRING FIELD (turn right over Thwaite Canal Bridge, Cragbank) are 5 small caves in the side of a little hill, which stands where a spring runs into the canal. No one told us what they were for when I was a child, and we did not go inside to investigate because they were dirty and very smelly - bed and breakfast accommodation (with en-suite facilities) for tramps like Scruffy Joe, a well known character.

An old map, indicating COKE OVENS, solved the problem. BEEHIVE SHAPED OVENS are to be found at intervals along the whole length of the canal.

The Five Beehive Coke Ovens
(Built around 1850) near the canal in The Spring Field.

(The next ones north of Carnforth are at Holme.) They were built around 1850 to produce coke which was in demand, especially for smithy work.

The ovens, in which coal was burned to produce the coke, were made of limestone blocks. Their interiors were about 7 feet in diameter and the domes were brick lined.

COAL BARGES towed by strong horses docked at a STONE-EDGED WHARF in the Spring Field. The quay is about 50 yards long and is still there, although it is now hidden by tall reeds. A sturdy wall can be seen at the canal side of the artificial hill, which is now covered with bushes and trees and looks quite natural.

This was once a busy place, with bargemen unloading coal and the keeper stoking up his five ovens. Quite likely he lived at a nearby old cottage and used the stream as his water supply.

In the 1920s, the SPRING FIELD was where crowds assembled for happy picnics and were entertained by our popular Brass Band, especially on Bank Holidays.

A favourite walk was 'Along-the- Banks-to-the-Spring-Field'. Watercress could be found in the spring and bunches of 'doddering' grass collected on the canal bank.

The Spring Field photographed with a BOX BROWNIE CAMERA in the early 1930s. There are no reeds and the stone-faced wharf can be seen.

At one time, OWD DEERFOOT lived in a hut in the Spring Field. He owned a donkey and cart, and went round Carnforth selling firewood. It is remembered that the donkey refused to go up Edward Street unless given a carrot by a lady who lived there.

EASTER-TIME brought jolly crowds to the Spring Field, where children loved to roll their PACE EGGS down its steep slope. Eggs, hard boiled and coloured with onion skins or cochineal (etc.) had been proudly on display on the ledges of sash windows.

A place of happy memories!

The Spring Field *(photographed in the 1990s)*
The artificial hill built to hold the 5 coke ovens is now overgrown by tall trees and bushes. Reeds hide a stone-faced wharf.

JAMES ERVING

In 1850, James Erving, aged 47, an industrialist and building contractor from Rochdale, came to Carnforth to retire. He settled at THWAITE HOUSE and became a gentleman farmer, running THWAITE FARM which was close by near the canal just over THWAITE BRIDGE (Cragbank).

He had three children:

1) A son who was in the merchant navy.

2) Another son, Henry Law Erving, who was in business as A MALTSTER in BOLTON-LE-SANDS.

3) A 10 year-old daughter, Jane, who was enrolled as a boarder at OWLET ASH SCHOOL, MILNTHORPE.

Thwaite Gate
James Erving's home, 1850 (Turn left over Thwaite Canal Bridge, Cragbank)

Tragedy befell son Henry. Just 10 months after their marriage, his wife died of consumption, and 6 months later he was found shot dead under a hedge near his malt kiln in TOWN END. (Someone who lived at THE OLD MALT HOUSE around 1975 was convinced that it was haunted.)

James Erving always liked to write things down and had recorded current events in Rochdale.

His retirement years in Carnforth gave him ample time to continue with his writings. He kept a MEMORANDUM in which he noted property prices and rentals etc. Later, he went on to record the activities of his neighbours, the affairs at his church and matters appertaining to local businesses.

He was a 'go-er' and a 'do-er', with a forceful character. He chaired committees and discoursed on local scandals, letting fly with his views whenever a good row broke out. Local people probably thought he was 'a reet busy-body and an awkud customer in tut bargain.'

He lived to be 84 and, no doubt, his long life contributed to the story of Carnforth.

[A lady named ANNE HYELMAN found Erving's MEMORANDUM in the Bookshop in Market Street and paid £20 for it, not many years ago. What a wonderful bargain!

Later she wrote an article called "A CARNFORTH CHRONICLE" which appeared in "LANCASHIRE LIFE". I am so glad I came upon it accidentally.]

As there was still no church here, James Erving had to attend services at WARTON. He probably jogged there with his bay pony, BROWN BILLY, which had cost him £24 10s 0d. When he sold it 2 years later, he only got £17 10s 0d (It seems that as a means of transport Brown Billy had depreciated, just like a modern car!)

Disagreements broke out at the church between the vicar, the choir and the organist. It was something about the singing and chanting of parts of the service. The year was 1857. Of course, James Erving joined in the trouble. He was against high church practices and chanting, and matters came to a head in 1865 when he had his BOOKS AND CUSHIONS removed from the church.

It is quite likely that, then and there, he made up his mind that he would work to get a church of its own built in Carnforth, because that is what he did - along with other important things.

After a long, eventful life, he was buried in the family grave in Warton Churchyard.

In his memorandum, he noted that in 1848 Carnforth consisted of:

28 Cottages
17 Farms
2 good houses
1 school
1 smithy
1 Methodist chapel
1 station (a halt)
3 pubs (Carnforth Inn; Golden Ball; Shovel Inn)

POPULATION

Carnforth's population increased by only 75 in the first half of the 19th century. In fact, during the 10 years from 1841 to 1851, it went down by 5.

This was proof that the coming of the canal, the increase in quarry work and the acquisition of a 'halt' on the Lancaster-Carlisle Railway had all had little effect on the growth of the small community.

A few more years were to pass before a rapid change took place. The GAZETTE, in 1863, reported on a speech given by the DEAN OF WARTON at a meeting at Carnforth. He pointed out to his audience that, although there were twice as many births registered as deaths, there had been little increase in the population during the last 20 years.

(In 1841, there were 299 people, and in 1861, there were 393)

The Dean suggested that the surplus must have been sent out as servants or had emigrated.

In later years, SMITHS the Newsagents and Printers in Market Street also became an Emigration Agency. Many were the local young men who fled overseas to Canada or Australia when they learnt that they had got some fair maiden INTO TROUBLE.

For large families living in small cottages, the answer to overcrowding was to put their children 'into service' as soon as possible. Before he was 13, my paternal grandfather was in service on a farm.

A LACK OF GOOD SAMARITANS

In the LANCASTER GUARDIAN of APRIL 8th 1854, Carnforth was reported as having shown a lack of loyalty and charity to "a soldier's wife, who started with severe labour pains whilst on a train journey from Glasgow to Sheffield." Her husband was one of a group of brave soldiers volunteering to serve abroad in the CRIMEAN WAR. Reluctantly, her husband had to leave her behind in Carnforth. The Station Master's wife had great difficulty in finding lodgings for the suffering woman. Eventually, a cottage owner agreed to take her in, but only after being guaranteed that all expenses would be paid.

THE PUBLIC HALL

Next to the SHOVEL INN and facing Kellet Road, a PUBLIC HALL was built around this period in time. It was used as the venue for social occasions of many sorts.

[During my childhood, other superior halls had taken over from it and I remember it being used only for the auctioning of household possessions when someone died, for visiting POT-FAIRS and for OIL-CLOTH AND LINOLEUM SALES. (Cheap-Jack Rubbish, according to local shop-keepers.)

Half of the old Public Hall was demolished recently but, in the part still standing, 2 built-up windows can still be seen and part of the doorway remains]

EDUCATION

In 1849, the DEAN AND CHAPTER OF WORCESTER, along with the REV GILBERT AINSLIE of Hall Garth (Over Kellet), Lord of the Manor, gave the tithe bam on flat ground at the top of Long Haws area to the township to be used for a school.

A one-storey building, with a bell-cote at the southern end, was opened in 1850, and was known as THE ENDOWED SCHOOL. It faced Lancaster Road, and a SCHOOL LANE led down to Long Haws.

The Old Endowed School on Lancaster Road
Willow Cottage and entrance to the School Lane on the right.

WILLOW COTTAGE was built close by as a home for the headmaster.

Twenty-five years later, when it was no longer occupied by school staff, a reporter from the

Lancaster Guardian wrote that it was a quaint-looking, one-storey building with a garden at the front and side. He added that a hospitable dame was living there.

[This small building still stands today, and has been altered little over the years. Until around 1940, it was a family dwelling, but since then it has been used as a storage-unit by a trading firm.]

RAILWAY DEVELOPMENT

Carnforth became a railway junction in 1857, when a single line was opened by THE FURNESS RAILWAY COMPANY between ULVERSTON and CARNFORTH - a distance of 19.5 miles. THE RIVER KENT at Arnside had been crossed by an imposing viaduct - quite an engineering feat.

In 1861, the main line, the Lancaster - Carlisle railway, was taken over by THE LONDON-NORTH-WESTERN RAILWAY (L.N.W.R.).

Carnforth was still "largely represented by green fields" when HARTLEYS, a well-known Kendal firm of Grocers, Bakers and Caterers, opened premises here near the small railway halt in 1863. They did a large trade in supplying food for gangs of men employed in converting the Furness Line from a single to a double track.

Also needing supplies were other workers, employed in the formidable task of connecting Carnforth with Wennington on the LEEDS TO LANCASTER MIDLAND LINE. The problem was that a tunnel 1230 yards long had to be dug at MELLING. The work was completed in 1866 and the new 9.5 mile track was opened by the FURNESS AND MIDLAND RAILWAY.

EDUCATION AGAIN

In January 1863, the LANCASTER GAZETTE reported the re-opening of the ENDOWED SCHOOL (at the present junction of Lancaster Road and Haws Hill). It had been closed for extensive work to be done to convert the original school into a large, L-shaped, 2-storey building, thus providing a lecture room which could later accommodate 250-300 people for worship.

To celebrate the event, a public tea party was held and about 150 people sat down to a "well-served and choice repast". The rooms had been lavishly decorated with wreaths of evergreens, flowers, festoons, arches, banners and a magnificent Egyptian canopy or tent.

In his address to the gathering, the DEAN OF WARTON stressed the importance of EDUCATION. He told of a young Carnforth man, 5ft 11ins tall, who was admitted to the Liverpool Police, but soon came home saying that he was "too short".

"Not in height," remarked the Dean, "but short in education!" He went on to say that the young Carnforthian could not read an address on an envelope, nor could he record his own proceedings in writing.

The Dean concluded his speech with an appeal to the good sense of Carnforth people to send their children to school regularly.

(Compulsory education was not introduced until 1870.)

Only twelve years after the school had been enlarged, a reporter from the Lancaster Guardian described it as, "rather an antique looking building, with diamond shaped panes in the windows."

CARNFORTH'S GROWTH

By 1863, the coming of the railways was having an effect on the growth of Carnforth.

Through the energy of two or three gentlemen, a GENERAL POST OFFICE was opened and the MONEY ORDER OFFICE became a boon to Carnforth and the surrounding district.

Also in 1863, "the little and unique town" put out an appeal for people to buy shares and set the work going for a new WORKINGMEN'S BUILDING SOCIETY near Robin Hill.

In October, the Gazette reported that 8 first-class houses were being built and also a grocer's shop and a tailoring establishment.

[Perhaps this was the beginning of STANLEY STREET, with Stephenson's and Bibby's the Grocers at one side and Murray's the Outfitters opposite.]

On October 24th, Carnforth's NEWSROOM AND LIBRARY (or Young Man's Mutual Improvement Society) was opened.

THE IRON WORKS

In the early 1860s, a group of Manchester businessmen, led by Herbert Walduck, was looking for a site for some new iron-works. Carnforth was chosen from the places under consideration because it offered the best facilities, e.g.:

1) A SUITABLE SITE alongside the road to Warton.

4) A GOOD PLACE on Warton shore for the DISPOSAL of waste products (slag) .

5) The FURNESS RAILWAY, along which phosphorus-free haematite IRON-ORE could be transported from an area around Ulverston.

6) THE L.N.W.R. and the MIDLAND RAILWAY could give access to the SOUTH LANCASHIRE and the YORKSHIRE coalfields respectively.

7) LIMESTONE quarried locally could act as flux in blast-furnaces.

8) The River Keer was nearby as a WATER SUPPLY.

Carnforth was heading to become an industrial centre when THE HAEMATITE IRON CO LTD was established in 1864, but what it lacked however was a good labour force. The population in 1861 was only 393. Some workers were employed by the railway companies and the rest were local men with an agricultural background or were quarrymen.

Carnforth Iron Works
Established 1864

SKILLED LABOUR was essential, so an agent was sent to the Midlands to recruit men. Because of a trade recession there, iron workers, particularly from DUDLEY, were willing to move to Carnforth to work. A few skilled men were also brought from South Wales and North-East England.

The Iron Works produced its first pig-iron from three blast furnaces in 1866.

Edward Barton started as an engineer and later became Managing Director. The company built him an imposing house - WARTON GRANGE.

The building firm of JOHN RIGG & SONS was founded in 1867 and its first contract was to start building terraces of houses for the new iron workers arriving locally. The chosen site was on a small hill on the Warton side of the River Keer. Its name was Millhead because, for many years, it had been the place where the Lord of Warton had corn-mills.

THE IRON WORKS company owned 2 private, narrow-gauge railway lines. One ran alongside Silverdale Road to Scout Quarry for limestone, and the other led to the tip on Warton Shore with wagonloads of hot slag.

THE 1870s

At the beginning of this decade, the Ironworks CHIMNEY was built. It soared 220ft into the air and became the area's most striking landmark. A correspondent of the LANCASTER GUARDIAN wrote, "I beheld the colossal chimney belching out perennially its smoke and fire like a young ETNA."

The town's own newspaper, the CARNFORTH GUARDIAN, reported in 1870: "CARNFORTH is taking strides towards FAME. It is preparing to make a stake among important manufacturing centres in North Lancashire."

Valuable assets were the railway-lines leading north, south, east and west. They set the scene for Carnforth to become an important junction. The small 'halt', along with the premises of Hartley's the Grocers, were demolished to make way for A NEW STATION. It had 2 platforms for L.N.W.R. traffic travelling North-South (Scotland-London), a 3rd platform for the FURNESS LINE to Barrow and a bay for trains travelling on the MIDLAND LINE to Leeds.

A photograph of the time showed a top-hatted station-master and bearded railway servants. A little wooden hut alongside Platform 1 was the POST OFFICE sorting department.

To cope with increased traffic, marshalling yards were built, also exchange sidings, wagon repair shops and a goods depot etc.

Carnforth Station built around 1870

Note: It has no frontage and Platform 1 has no cover. The bridge is the present one on the Carnforth - Warton Road. The small wooden building on the right was the Post Office.

Each of the three railway companies had its own locomotive shed where its engines (in a distinctive livery) were 'garaged', repaired and prepared for journeys.

Initialled uniform buttons showed for which particular company the railwaymen worked. The men were extremely loyal to their own companies.

I am proud of my little collection of family buttons. Like many others, mine was certainly a RAILWAY FAMILY. We had steam chuffing through our veins!

GRANDFATHERS:

1. A MIDLAND RAILWAY SIGNALMAN. Originally a porter at Leeds, Shipley, Eldroth and finally

Carnforth Box near the Midland Station.

2. A GOODS GUARD ON THE L.N.W.R. (a 'Wessie'-man). Once an agricultural labourer at Scorton.

FATHER:

An engine driver (eventually) after climbing the railway ladder: (1) Knocker-up (2) Engine cleaner (3) Fireman (4) Driver.

UNCLES:

7 of them, all footplate-men, employed by one or other of the three companies.

Family discussions always led to claims as to whose 'Line' was the BEST.

MY HUSBAND'S MATERNAL GRANDPARENTS came to live here via the Furness Railway.

Many of Carnforth's Senior Citizens are living here because their grandparents were attracted to this locality in order to work on the railway.

To accommodate the increasing number of their employees, the Railway Companies found it necessary to build houses for them to rent.

Eventually the following places appeared on the scene at Carnforth:

GROSVENOR PLACE, MIDLAND TERRACE, THE CANAL COTTAGES, KEER VILLAS and A TERRACE IN CRAGBANK.

CENSUS

In the CENSUS OF 1871, there was a population of 1091. The count had almost TREBLED IN 10 YEARS due to the influx of new workers.

THE CANAL COTTAGES and HALL STREET were mentioned in the census returns, but addresses were not given. The names of most inhabitants were followed by "village" as their place of residence. Amongst people named were:

1) Arthur Threlfall - music teacher.

2) John Rigg - mason and bricklayer.

3) John Smith & wife - schoolmaster and mistress.

2 families were registered as canal-boat people and one person was registered as a straw-plaiter.

THE GAS WORKS

An auspicious event of 1871 was the promotion of Carnforth's GAS WORKS. They were situated on land between Lancaster Road and the canal basin, where coal barges were unloaded. The manager lived in the GAS HOUSE alongside Lancaster Road and eventually people paid their gas bills at offices there. Edward Barton and James Erving were among the directors of the company.

The following year, AN AMMONIACAL MANUFACTORY was built near the Gas Works.

THE IRON WORKS AGAIN

At this time, there was a great demand for STEEL both in Britain and abroad. The rapid development of railways had a need for rails, axles etc.

At the Ironworks, TWO CONVERTERS were built in 1871. Two years later steel plate and rail mills were installed.

ACCOMMODATION FOR IRON WORKERS

100 new houses had been built in Millhead by 1872: Mary Street, William Street and Albert Street. Were these perhaps the names of Edward Barton's family?

Red Court

Built for one of Edward Barton's family. It became a restaurant and at present is The Working Men's Club.

Carnforth's RED COURT was built for another member of Barton's family and streets for workers arrived on the scene here eventually:

1) HALL ST, named after a company director, was for foremen. It became known as THE PIG AND PIANO ROW - a pig-sty in the garden and a status-symbol PIANO in the PARLOUR. Later its name was changed to BESSEMER TERRACE after Sir Henry Bessemer, a Victorian engineer who had pioneered BLAST FURNACES in 1856. (He also invented a non-rolling saloon for ships, to prevent sea-sickness ... but that's a different story.)

2) A row of houses opposite the church became known as PIG-LIFTERS ROW, because the men living there had bent backs through lifting the very heavy iron bars (pigs) or so it was said!

3) POND STREET, POND TERRACE and RAMSDEN STREET were for labouring workmen. These houses became known as Carnforth's Lake district, a derogatory term because of the pond there (remember TOAD PLUD?)

RELAXATION FOR OUR GROWING POPULATION

The Lancaster Guardian of May 11th 1872 recorded the first meeting of Carnforth's new CRICKET CLUB. It is said that Dr Jackson donated the field to the town, the one that is in use today. At a later date, an adjoining BOWLING GREEN was made.

RELIGIOUS AFFAIRS OF THE DECADE

In 1869, James Erving had written to the Ecclesiastical Committee and had obtained a grant of £120 per annum to pay the stipend for a curate in Carnforth.

The REV J A FIDLER had been appointed, and started services in the Lecture Room above the Endowed School. Initially he lived in lodgings but eventually, along with his wife and a servant, he moved into CARNFORTH LODGE, which faces Lancaster Road and was handy for the school building. The road outside his home sloped down to the foot of Huthwaite and became known as FIDLER'S HILL (a term STILL used by Old Carnforthians.)

John Fidler was the first vicar, a position he held from 1869 to 1897.

James Erving was one of a committee of 3 responsible for initiating the building of CHRIST CHURCH. Public meetings were held to raise money and, at the beginning of the 'seventies', a start was made and a site purchased.

James Erving disagreed with the design of the altar and had an aggravating time with the Reverend Fidler. When he found out that musical services were to be the rule in the new church, he declared that he would take no further part in its activities.

The church, strongly built of stone in the 'decorated' style of architecture, was completed in

1873 and consecrated on August 14th of that year. It had cost £2,200, raised by subscriptions and a grant from the Church Building Society.

There was seating accommodation for 328 worshippers, but that soon became inadequate because Carnforth was growing so rapidly.

This first church building was described as "rather small and unpretentious". Its opening led to the break-away from Warton and to Carnforth becoming a parish in its own right. But for another 50 years Carnforthians were buried in Warton Churchyard.

THE WESLEYAN METHODISTS

A report in the Lancaster Guardian of April 26th 1873 stated that, after a tea party and public meeting, the Methodist's FOUNDATION STONE was laid. This was for their new chapel on LANCASTER ROAD which would provide seating for 250 worshippers. The old Presbyterian Chapel behind the Shovel Inn had become too small for increasing congregations.

[There appears to be some confusion about the year of the opening. The Mannex Directories record it as 1870.]

LOCAL NEWSPAPER REPORTS

During 1875, several reports about Carnforth appeared in the Lancaster Guardian which illustrated how it was quickly changing from a quiet little village into a busy town.

In the issue of July 3rd, a correspondent wrote that he had often passed through Carnforth's busy railway yards and thought that they gave the impression of a busy, pushing place. He decided to alight at the station and learn more about the town. He had a talk with the man in charge of the W H SMITH BOOKSTALL and that cynical man remarked that if anyone could see anything in Carnforth worth the attention of a sentient being, it was more than he could!

The correspondent described Carnforth as a straggling hybrid village with some houses very old and some very new. (There were 1,100 inhabitants in that year.) He said that some streets had been erected in the upper part of the village: "Cosy, snug-looking cribs with that delightful addition of a patch of flower-garden in front."

Some streets had been named in ambitious style, e. g. OXFORD STREET, and STANLEY STREET. From the school to the main body of the village, one side of the highroad, Lancaster Road, was lined with terraces of houses of better class, which had a good view of the Cumbrian range of hills and the crag at Warton.

In another issue of the Lancaster Guardian, a reporter wrote that he had heard that Carnforth was a rising place with a power of expansion such as that which had transformed, with magic rapidity, the township of BARROW.

WOULD CARNFORTH GROW TO THE SIZE OF BARROW?

That was a problem for builders. To provide for such an eventuality, they started to build some streets with one or two houses at each end so that, at some future date, the spaces between could be filled in, e. g. PRESTON STREET.

Along LANCASTER ROAD and SCOTLAND ROAD, houses at the ends of terraces were left with alternate stones protruding from the frontage to facilitate the building-on of more houses later. (Some of these can still be seen today. Others were chipped off as they provided a dangerous challenge to potential young mountaineers.)

One solitary house (now next to the library) was ready to receive neighbours on both sides. None arrived.

HAWK STREET could have had 30-40 houses, but there was no extension to the 4 which were first built.

The extent to which Carnforth would ultimately grow was still not apparent.

Another correspondent of the Lancaster Guardian wrote an article about his impression of Carnforth people. To him, the bulk of the population seemed to be "working-class, thrifty, orderly and well conditioned". He went on to say they had a thriving independent look and the majority showed evidence that they earned their living by the sweat of brow and body in the big, hot manufactory in the centre of the village.

"The furnaces cast up fumes of fire," he wrote, "and workers earn whatever they are paid."

THE WATER SUPPLY

A 3rd newspaper report of 1875 concerned the supply of water for the growing population, and the problem of sewage disposal.

It stated that Carnforth people were in great straits for water. There was no branch of Lancaster's Waterworks in the town and its few pumps yielded a meagre, and not very drinkable, supply of water. Many householders had provided themselves with capacious rain-tubs so that the spouts on their housetops served a useful purpose, e.g. THE DOLLY TUB ROW AT CRAGBANK.

'THE CLOUDS OF HEAVEN' were the direct source of Carnforth's water supply. They were looked upon as precious and practical rather than as poetical things.

SEWAGE

Around this time, main drains had been laid in some areas of Carnforth and a sewage disposal tank had been built on the Marsh, near the River Keer. Unfortunately water was not available to flush the sewers. Canal water had been considered but the canal company would have asked for payment and engineering work would have been necessary to lift the water - as high as 70 feet in some areas. Moreover, it was unlikely that the canal could provide a sufficient supply of water.

THE POST OFFICE

Between 1878 and 1879, the Post Office building was much enlarged and Carnforth became an important postal centre for a wide area as far as Ingleton and Kirkby Lonsdale.

Beside the railway line at Cragbank, a special device was built which enabled express trains to pick up Carnforth's mailbags without decelerating.

THE IRON WORKS

Science had progressed and, in 1879, the need for phosphorus-free iron-ore in blast furnaces no longer applied. This meant that Carnforth lost the advantage it had enjoyed with its good local supply from the Furness District and trade was adversely affected from then on.

RIGGS THE BUILDERS

In 1878, Riggs built several houses at the bottom of Hewthwaite, but could not add to the terrace because they had their joinery shop and sawmill there. It became necessary for them to find new premises.

HEWTHWAITE TERRACE was not completed for 5 years. The date on the top house is 1883 (now a veterinary surgery).

Hewthwaite Terrace
Coal Wharf on the right. Gas House bottom right.
Iron Works chimney in the background.

RIGGS' NEW YARD was opened on land at the bottom of Oxford Street, and a large Joiners' Shop was built with circular saws, hand saws, a planning and thicknessing machine, and an upright spindle moulding machine.

There was a great demand for building material at the time and the yard was a busy place, selling cement, plaster, drainpipes, chimney-pots, slop-stones, bricks, lathes, lime, hair etc.

THE 1880s

In spite of fluctuating trade, 6 blast furnaces were operating at the IRON WORKS in 1880, and their tall chimney was enthusiastically puffing long ribbons of smoke over Carnforth.

As the town's importance as a BUSY RAILWAY JUNCTION developed, the population continued to grow.

The streets echoed to the whistle and whoosh of express trains and to the puffing and the chuffing of shunt-engines as they clanked wagons back and forth in the busy marshalling yards.

The Mannex Directory of 1881 stated that a large, new and IMPORTANT STATION had just been completed at a cost of £40,000. Platform 1 had been roofed over and a ticket office, passengers' waiting rooms and a parcels' office had been built with an imposing stone façade.

Passengers alighting here were very impressed with the grandeur of Carnforth Station's new appearance.

THE STATION HOTEL

(Opposite the main station entrance)

This prestigious building was one of the finest hotels in Northern England.

Samuel Mercer, the victualler, was in charge of

Market Street, *formerly Main Street. Looking down to the Station Hotel. Photographed around 1890*

'posting', and visitors could hire coaches to take them to beauty spots in the local countryside. Picnic and wedding parties could be catered for on the shortest notice.

The hotel's name, on a huge roof-level hoarding, could be read by passengers in trains. Some people broke the long journey between London and Scotland by staying overnight at the hotel.

The main entrance was on the corner of the building facing the station. Railinged steps, with a lamp at each side, led up to the doorway, and the hotel's name was chiselled in the stone-work over it.

A NEW CHAPEL AND SCHOOL

A move by the people of the EMMANUEL CONGREGATION faith in 1880 led to Carnforth acquiring a new place of worship and a new school. A CHAPEL SCHOOL, costing £850, was built at the top of an incline leading off HAWK STREET. Up to this time, services had been held in a room over a stable behind the Carnforth Inn. Seamstresses had once used the stable-room.

The new CHAPEL SCHOOL could seat 250 worshippers for Sunday services. On weekdays it was used as a school. Children were given an education, free from Church of England teachings, at this BRITISH SCHOOL.

The Chapel School
Built in 1892 by people of the Emmanuel Congregational Faith. It became known as The British School.

The architect of the building was called Mr Oliver. He had given his services free so, in gratitude, the road leading up to it became known as Oliver Street, a name which fell into disuse.

HARTLEY'S THE GROCERS

The first shop which Hartley's opened in this area was pulled down along with the small railway "halt" when the land was cleared for building the new station.

Lancaster Road
Looking toward Hartley's shop at the cross-roads.

The firm then built a large shop and bakery in Millhead at the corner of Carlisle Terrace with Warton Road, and also opened a fine new shop at the crossroads in Carnforth. John Hartley & Co were advertised as 'GROCERS, BAKERS, CONFECTIONERS, FLOUR AND PROVENDER DEALERS'. They also became well-known as the best catering firm in the district.

Hartley's soon became the busiest shop in town, and Carnforth's first local telephone was installed when the firm's 2 shops were connected in 1881.

CARNFORTH'S GROWTH

The population had reached almost 2,000 when the census was taken in 1881, and Carnforth was still growing and developing. In the TOPOGRAPHY AND DIRECTORY OF LANCASTER AND 16 MILES AROUND, P MANNEX wrote:

"CARNFORTH is a flourishing village at the junction of the FURNESS AND MIDLAND RAILWAY with the L.N.W. R."

THE CENSUS OF 1881

It is interesting to take a mental stroll with the man who, over 100 years ago, went round the town recording the names of people living in the houses which had been built by 1881.

Start by THWAITE CANAL BRIDGE at Cragbank and remain on that side of the road:

> THWAITE HOUSE
> BESSEMER TERRACE
> COAL WHARF
> STANLEY STREET AND HILL STREET
>   (22 houses)
> OXFORD STREET (18 houses)

Up Lower OLD ROAD (14 houses)
North Rd? HOLLIBANK COTTAGES
                    KELLET ROAD (17 houses)
                    RUSSELL DRIVE

Turn &
come back
	HIGHFIELD TERRACE (1 block, 21
	    houses)
	BOOKER TERRACE (10 houses)
	CANAL TERRACE (6 houses)
	CANAL HOUSE
	OLD CHAPEL HOUSE (Tin-plate
	    worker)
	CHAPEL COTTAGE (Elizabeth
	    Walmsley, Local dealer)
	BANK COTTAGE (Ellen Jackson,
	    Lodging house keeper)

Up Higher
North Rd
	OLD COACH ROAD
	MOUNT TERRAGE (10 houses)
	OLD COACH ROAD
	THOMSPSON'S FARM & TOWN END
	    FARM
	STANKELL HOUSE (James Morrison)
	HARDACRE HOUSE (John Mashiter)
	HALL GOWAN FARM (Thomas
	    Jackson, Farmer)
	HALL CROFT COTTAGE
	HALL GOWAN COTTAGE
	HALL GOWAN (Robert Jackson,
	    gentleman)
	OLD COACH ROAD (No.s 18, 19, & 20)
	CARNFORTH HOUSE (Robert
	    Sturzaker)
	CARNFORTH COTTAGE (William
	    Hornby, Railway labourer)
	OLD COACH ROAD (Up to number 45)

Now Upper Market St	ALMA TERRACE 9A LANCASTER ROAD (George Hartley, Grocer) LANCASTER ROAD (to no. 19) HIGH BANK
Shore area	MARSH COTTAGES (No 1, Locomotive Driver, No 2, Railway guard) MARSH GATE FARM MARSH HOUSE (Rowlandson, farmer) CRAGG BANK COTTAGES (20) THE HOLLIES (Mr Woodroofe, retired farmer) CROTCHET TERRACE (2 houses) Later called Hope Terrace? TRAVELLERS REST (William Sarginson, innkeeper) LANCASTER ROAD (No.s 13-1) THE LODGE (John Fidler, perpetual curate, his sister and servant) WILLOW COTTAGE (Family of 6) FAIR VIEW POLICE STATION LANCASTER ROAD CHURCH STREET (1 & 2) CARNFORTH INN (Mr Brocklebank) SCOTLAND ROAD (Henry Murray, saddler) SCOTLAND ROAD (Richard Bibby) NEWS ROOM FREE TRADE BUILDING (Stephenson's big family)

Now	MAIN STREET
Market St	QUEEN'S HOTEL (John Batty, Licensed Victualler)

FREE TRADE BUILDINGS (4 houses)
CARNFORTH HALL (Wm Hainsworth, Contractor, family of 8 & servant)
MAIN STREET (2 houses)
VICTORIA PLACE
MAIN STREET (Edward Whinray)
STATION HOTEL (Samuel Mereer, proprietor)
NEW STREET (19 houses)
THE HAWS (private school)
EDWARD STREET (No.s 1 & 2)
MAIN STREET (8 Wilkinsons in a family)
REFRESHMENT ROOM
CARNFORTH STATION
MIDLAND TERRACE (12 houses)
1 KEER BANK

That was the whole of Carnforth.

THE HAWS was a private boarding school for girls before the terrace of houses, called HAWS HILL was built.

In 1881, MISS EMMA PICKFORD was recorded as the teacher there, with Miss Ann Hutton (aged 24), a boarder assistant, 5 scholars and a servant. Miss Pickford was the daughter of Cornelius Pickford, a manure dealer. In the Parish Church, she is

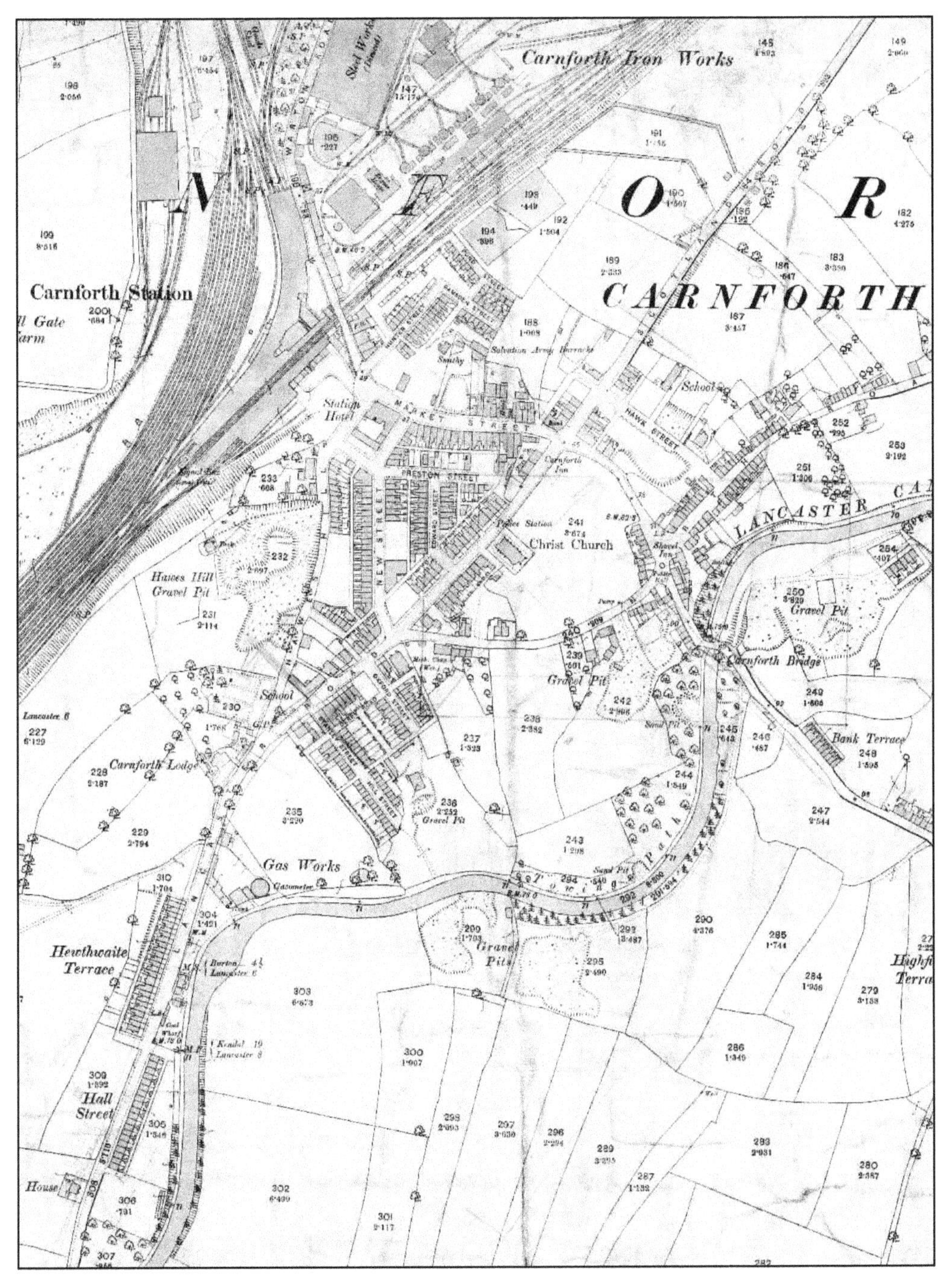

OS Map of Carnforth c. 1890

commemorated by a stained-glass window which portrays Jesus surrounded by children.

Also in 1881, DR EDWARD JACKSON was named as a surgeon. Later he became the Medical Officer and Public Vaccinator.

His surgery was at ROBIN HILL, Market Street, and there he pulled out teeth and snipped off tonsils and adenoids.

His patients were fascinated by the many glass-fronted cases of stuffed birds and animals which lined the walls of his waiting room.

LAW AND ORDER

In 1881, a fine new POLICE STATION was built on Lancaster Road opposite the Parish Church. The "massive work" was undertaken by Thomas Peel of Cragg Bank.

Generations of Carnforth children were to creep on velvet tip-ties (toes?) when passing this building, because they believed it had dark, underground dungeons in which they would be locked up and fed dark diet of dry bread and water if they were disobedient and naughty.

A policeman on his beat became a familiar and much respected member of the community. People felt safe and secure as he patrolled the streets during the hours of darkness. Just the mention of his name by parents was an effective deterrent to disruptive youngsters.

Two other types of workers walked the streets at night:

1) The young "KNOCKERS-UP" on their rounds to awaken railwaymen who were due on duty.

2) The LAMP-LIGHTER. This was a new occupation in Carnforth. GAS pipes had been laid and lampposts erected in the principal streets for a wonderful event. At 6pm on October 11th 1883, the great switch-on took place. Carnforth was lit-up!

CARNFORTH'S ARCHITECTURE

Roof of the bank at the cross-roads.
An example of Carnforth's architecture with rounded corners.

Carnforth is often dismissed as an ugly, grey little town, and its inhabitants do not always dispute that. People tend to walk around familiar places with their gaze fixed at eye-level. An upward glance can frequently reveal pleasant architectural designs.

Among those who have looked upon the town favourably was a young architect educated at Aberdeen University who lived and worked locally in the 1980s. His opinion was that it is an interesting small town with some well-designed buildings.

Back of the same bank, *viewed from Booth's Supermarket car park. Note the arch supporting the tall chimney stack.*

It may be assumed that one Victorian architect was responsible for all the buildings with attractively "ROUNDED CORNERS", which took up their positions in Carnforth during the 1870s and 1880s:

   1) THE STATION HOTEL

   2) STATION BUILDINGS (Seen by passengers

84

leaving the station)

3) THE BANK (with balustrade)

4) HARTLEY'S SHOP (Both at the crossroads)

5) THE COUNCIL CHAMBERS

6) THE TOP OF NEW STREET

A FAMOUS "PASSER-THROUGH"

In Sept 1883, many Carnforthians assembled on the station to cheer and wave to the famous politician, Mr GLADSTONE ("a grand fella!"), who was en route by train to Barrow-in-Furness. He graciously acknowledged their greetings.

BUSY RAIL TRAFFIC

As people began to find rail travel convenient and reasonably cheap (especially for railway employees), visitors came to Carnforth from all the surrounding district.

Special trains were put on for particular events such as that, in 1883, when a big, 4-day Sale of Work was held in a large marquee. Crowds arrived from Lancaster, Morecambe and villages all around at cheap excursion rates. The event raised the magnificent sum of £70.

Ten years later a similar 3-day sale was organised, but disappointingly raised only £25 and a number of the articles were not sold. *[It still happens!]*

EDUCATION AGAIN

The old Endowed School became known as the NATIONAL SCHOOL. The year 1883 is engraved in the stonework under the bell-cote. It must refer to when further extension work was done, after that undertaken in 1863.

When Christ Church was built, the large lecture room in the school, used for religious services, had become free for the use of more classrooms. Eventually the school could accommodate 500 scholars.

THE CO-OP ARRIVED

Lancaster C.W.S. (Co-operative Wholesale Society) saw Carnforth as a potential place in which to spread its new ideas of retail trade. The SKERTON CO-OP opened a branch shop here, which soon showed profits.

In 1885, a group of Carnforth people met in the Iron Works Room and decided that the town should have a society of its own. A site was chosen in Market Street and, later that year, a shop was opened with a membership of 174 and a share capital of £450.

My paternal grandparents must have been among the original members because their 'check-number' was 52.

To increase enrolment, each new member was given a solid silver teaspoon with the year 1885 and the society's emblem embossed on the handle.

[At the society's Diamond Jubilee, in 1960, Carnforth Co-op had 6,172 members and a share capital of £500,000.]

The Co-op had arrived and Hartley's found they had a powerful rival.

THE SALVATION ARMY

1886 was the year when the SALVATION ARMY was established in Carnforth. At the outset, services were held in the upper part of a wooden, barn-like building which stood on spare land between Hunter Street and Ramsden Street.

It is thought that DOCKRAYS (com & flour merchants and hay & straw dealers) stabled their cart-horses in the lower part of the building.

Later, the Salvation Army moved to premises in PRESTON STREET.

ON THE POLITICAL FRONT

In 1887, the CONSERVATIVE CLUB was opened. This fine building, in STATION BUILDINGS, had a well equipped billiards and reading-room.

Not to be outdone, on August 27 of the same year, THE LIBERALS opened a club in a building at the top of Stanley Street (now a launderette).

There was no Labour Party.

THE MARKET

Local farmers and gardeners sold their produce at a MARKET held, each Monday, on spare land at the bottom of Market Street (named Main Street in the census of 1881).

PUBLICITY

In May 1887, a new publication made its appearance on the local news front. THE CARNFORTH MONTHLY REMINDER, which advertised local shops and train timetables, was printed, published and distributed FREE by W J WEEKS, printer and billposter, 38 Market Street. He also printed THE CARNFORTH WEEKLY NEWS, which cost one penny per copy.

SHOPPING

Butter was advertised at 1s 4d per lb (pound), potatoes at 1s 0d per stone, apples at 2d per lb and eggs at 1d each. This was at the time when workmen's wages were counted in shillings, not pounds, per week.

At a shop in Victoria Buildings (bottom of New Street facing the Station Hotel), men's suits cost between 17s 6d and £1.

At the Coal Wharf near the Canal Basin, coal was sold at 7d per cwt sack. Most houses in Carnforth had cellars and loads of coal were delivered by horse-and-cart and dropped down the holes near front doors.

THE QUEEN - GOD BLESS HER!

Queen Victoria's Golden Jubilee, in 1887, was celebrated in Carnforth with an ever-popular Field Day, and the distribution of commemorative mugs to the children. *[I have one, given to my father who was one year old.]*

All the local villages over a wide area held Village Fetes to celebrate the Queen's important occasion, and HARTLEY'S were able to cater for them all on the same day.

HARTLEY'S RIVAL

CARNFORTH CO-OPERATIVE SOCIETY prospered and grew. The aim of the Movement (which started in Rochdale) was to cater for all aspects of its members' lives and deaths, e. g. feed and clothe them from specialist shops, rent and furnish homes for them, provide for their social lives, for banking, insurance, funerals etc.

The Society built-up all the top left-hand side of NEW STREET and, in 1888, the magnificent CO-OPERATIVE HALL was opened. Along with OFFICES and a BOARD ROOM, it extended over 4 shops (BOOT & SHOE, LARGE GROCERY DEPARTMENT, BUTCHERY & CONFECTIONERY) and a big warehouse.

The Co-Operation Hall accommodated 550 people for all Carnforth's main social events, balls, whist-drives, concerts, conversaziones, agricultural shows etc.

Tower and Spire of the CWS building in New Street
Below the offices and the fine HALL were 4 busy shops.
The Reading Room was behind the top-most window.

From a tiled entrance, two staircases led up to the hall, which had a gallery, a stage and an ante-room with kitchen facilities. A door from the kitchen opened on to a spiral staircase, leading from an outside door in John Street up to a Reading Room FOR MEN on the top floor. (John Street leads from the top of New Street to Edward Street and Preston Street.) It can be assumed that women were not expected to have time for reading!

Newspapers and magazines were spread out on a large table. Chairs (with arm-rests!) and a warm, open fire welcomed the men after their exhausting climb.

On special days, Union Jacks were flown proudly

from flagpoles on top of the fine spire and the tower, which beautified the splendid New Street premises of Carnforth's Co-operative Society.

In Market Street two large shops were opened:

1) THE DRAPERY DEPARTMENT, including clothes for ladies and gentlemen (suits made to measure).

2) THE FURNISHING AND HARDWARE DEPARTMENT.

The Quarterly dividend, paid out to members from the Society's profits, was a great incentive for people to "SHOP AT THE CO-OP".

THE 1890s

This last decade of the nineteenth century saw the completion of streets which form the nucleus of Carnforth.

Travel by train to Lancaster and Morecambe was cheap and reliable, but people had no need to leave Carnforth to go shopping. Our two main streets had an excellent range of specialist shops which could supply all requirements.

There was no shortage of work for men. Women were expected to stay at home and look after their families.

Carnforthians worked hard and played hard.

Special events, such as the UNITED GALA of 1890, were supported by the whole community.

Galas and Field Days tended to follow a set formula: Assembly on the Market Ground, a Parade round the town led by the excellent Brass Band, and on to a field (perhaps Sandford's or Slinger's up North Road) where Fancy Dress Competitions, races and sporting events were held.

The bandsmen, looking smart in uniform, were led by Mr F Greenland. They had been playing together for a while, because it was mentioned in the press that they had entertained at a Regatta at Arnside in 1887.

AN AUSPICIOUS EVENT

When a fine new horse-drawn FIRE ENGINE was presented to the town in 1890, among the dignitaries present were MR DAN MILLER, the school-master, and MR FARNWORTH, the Station Master. A photograph of the event was taken in front of the station.

The modern steam engine was kept in a shed at the rear of the QUEEN'S HOTEL and it had a fire laid ready to light immediately a call for action was received. Two large black horses belonging to the hotel were then hitched to the appliance and driven off at a furious pace either up or down MARKET STREET.

The same horses were used to pull a glass-sided hearse.

THE QUEEN'S HOTEL advertised "Posting" in all its branches: hearses, mourning coaches, wedding carriages etc. It had stabling for 40 horses.

The hotel had good accommodation for visitors and was well-known for selling wines and spirits of finest quality and ales and stouts in good condition. Cigars of choicest brands were sold.

(Photographs of important events were taken by MR THOMAS RATHBONE, a decorator of Hawk Street. He was a man of many talents and one of them was for music. He held "Tonic-sol-fah" classes and his pupils put on entertaining concerts.)

WAYSIDE REFRESHMENT FOR ANIMALS

A water trough for horses, with a low one alongside for dogs, was situated at the junction of Warton and Keer Roads.

[The troughs became neglected & overgrown and my husband had to pull away weeds and branches before he could photograph them in 1990. Recently they have been renovated.]

THE CENSUS OF 1891

The census returns of 1891 indicate how the town had developed during the 10 years since the count of 1881.

New streets had been built, namely: HAWS HILL (up to number 25), BOOTH STREET, PRESTON STREET, HUNTER STREET, RAMSDEN STREET, POND STREET and HEWTHWAITE TERRACE (up to no. 25).

EDWARD STREET had been completed from 2 houses to 28.

Bessemer Terrace had been renamed HALL STREET.

HIGHFIELD LANE had been added to Highfield Terrace, forming a second terrace of houses.

Four more houses had been built on to the two in Crochet Terrace, which then changed its name to HOPE TERRACE.

Hope Terrace

NEW STREET had 44 houses instead of the original 19.

THE OLD COACH ROAD had changed its name to NORTH ROAD, and MAIN STREET had become MARKET STREET.

For the first time, THE GAS HOUSE is recorded (because Carnforth had acquired gas street lights).

THE NURSERIES are also mentioned. (These were an early form of garden-centre. Now the residence is a private house, number 182 Lancaster Road.)

The spelling of some names had changed, e.g. AYR TARN became HARE TARN, and PLAINTREE

HOUSE became PLANETREE HOUSE, probably because many names had been passed on only by word of mouth.

Also mentioned are:

LAUND HOUSE (Lancaster Road near Stanley Street junction) and REDCAR HOUSE. These detached residences became the homes of some of the town's important persons.

THE TEMPERANCE HOTEL, Preston Street, where the guests could be safe from the demon drink.

[I recall two other such hotels, one on Scotland Road and the other in Lower New Street, which had signs on boards above their front doors.]

A CANAL BOAT: Captain Bramwell and his wife. Crew: their son Robert.

THE HOLLIES: Cragg Bank was occupied by John Erving (born in Rochdale) and 2 servants: Edward Wilkinson and Elizabeth. *[It would appear that John Erving (son of James) willed "The Hollies" to his servant, who later named his son Erving Wilkinson.]*

OXFORD HOUSE: Number 1 Oxford Street was the home of John Rigg and his family (The Builders).

MARKET STREET: No. 4 was occupied by Dr Edward Jackson, his sons, Edward and William, and daughters, Nelly and Nora. Also 2 servants.

[Numerous homes had servants.]

Market Street
Looking up towards Hartley's shop at the crossroads.
Dr Jackson's home and surgery on the left.

No. 29 was the home of a butcher, John Williams. His son, William Williams, inherited his father's business and became the well-known character, "Butcher Billy", who went round killing house-holders' pigs to order.

The record shows that, in addition to their large families of 6, 7 or more, some householders took in half-a-dozen or so boarders to increase their incomes. EDWARD STEET, NEW STREET, ALMA TERRACE, SCOTLAND ROAD AND NORTH ROAD had the most over-crowded houses. The situation was eased in those houses in Scotland Road & New Street, which had attics.

A WELL-KNOWN CHARACTER

Towns are not just a collection of buildings and

businesses, but are also made up of the people who live there. Many people "keep themselves to themselves", die and are forgotten by all except their immediate family. Others have strong personalities and are remembered for years and years by whole communities.

Headmaster Dan Miller with a class of boys *around 1896 at the National School (formerly Endowed School, later Church of England)*

Back Row: *Sam Howie, Dick Woodhouse, next 2 unknown, George Davies, Billy Harrison*

Middle Row: *Bill Martin, Dick Haycock, unknown, Harvey Hunter, Maurice King, Lewis McDonald, Tom Clark*

Front Row: *Jim Mason, Bill Marsden, Billy Jackson, Tom Bagguley, Tom Wilkinson, Taylor Rigg, Mason Simpson*

One such person was MR DAN MILLER, headmaster of the NATIONAL (FORMERLY ENDOWED) SCHOOL who believed in strict discipline. *[Both my parents vouched for that!]*

He took an active part in all that was going on in Carnforth. His home was PLANE TREE HOUSE in LOWER NORTH ROAD, which became known as MILLER'S LANE because of its famous resident. Even to this day, the slope leading from his house up to the junction with Kellet Road is recognised by all true Carnforthians as MILLER'S HILL.

Around 1890, the barn-like building near Plane Tree House on Miller's Lane was in use as a factory. Seven or eight males were employed in the production of wooden doorknobs *[now opposite the C of E School]*.

THOSE CATERERS AGAIN

HARTLEY'S efficiency was given a unique test when, at one hour's notice, they were asked to supply sustenance for a whole regiment of Highland troops during a certain night at Lancaster station. The soldiers were en route to Egypt (which Britain had occupied in 1882).

Hartley's passed the test with flying colours (and NO sliced bread)!

On occasions, they supplied for as many as 6,000 people at High Sherriffs' fêtes.

RELIGIOUS MATTERS

Religious fervour abounded in the town and, due to the ever-increasing population, the 4 places of worship were packed on Sundays.

THE PARISH CHURH was proving to be too small and there were complaints about over-crowding. It was said that people were often ill through the crush! It was necessary to use both exit doors.

People of the EMMANUEL CONGREGATIONAL faith realised that they had outgrown their Chapel School when, in 1892, the huge crowd of people eager to attend the HARVEST FESTIVAL could not all get into the building. This was an important service, when a choir of 40 voices was accompanied by an orchestra.

THE SUNDAY SCHOOL was also very well attended. 1892 was the year when 200 children and 100 parents were taken on a Summer Outing to Sandside. At 11.30am, they all assembled at the Chapel School and marched in procession to the station, singing hymns. They had a happy time in Sandside and enjoyed bags of food and cups of tea, before returning to Carnforth on their special train.

THE SOUND OF MUSIC

Music echoed through the town when THE IRONWORKS BAND of 1895 added to the sound of the Brass Band, which eventually had a wooden BAND ROOM, down by the canal near Kellet Road Bridge.

The rousing music of the SALVATION ARMY BAND also added to the oom-pah-pah a few years later.

THE COUNCIL

1895 saw the constitution of the URBAN COUNCIL, which consisted of 9 distinguished gentlemen of the community.

The motto which they strove for was: "EFFICIENCY WITH ECONOMY."

A fine, horse-drawn AMBULANCE was presented to the council at the occasion when it attained urban status.

THE CO-OP AGAIN

Trade increased at the 6 departmental shops in New Street and Market Street, and a delivery service was kept very busy taking groceries by horse-and-cart to the homes of members.

The Society was doing so well in 1896 that BRANCH SHOPS were opened in surrounding villages: MILLHEAD, WARTON, BOLTON-LE-SANDS, HOLME, SILVERDALE, ARNSIDE and even across the bay at GRANGE, LINDALE, ALLITHWAITE and GRANGE FELL.

CARNFORTHIANS BECAME MOBILE

THE CARNFORTH CYCLE COMPANY was established in 1896 by Mr Charles Dean, at an old white-washed building on Lancaster Road, adjacent to the Carnforth Inn.

A few years later the firm was turning out over 100 new cycles per annum.

CYCLING became a very popular form of recreation. MAN was abandoning 'Shank's pony' and speeding off on WHEELS (only 2 so far at Carnforth).

CHURCH AFFAIRS AGAIN

THE "CONGS"

In 1896, a crowd of 1,000 people was present for the laying of the Foundation Stone for a new Emmanuel CONGREGATIONAL CHURCH in Hawk Street.

117 families were connected with the Chapel and 270 children attended the Sunday School. The "CONGS" were very strong in their faith!

After the stone-laying ceremony, the Brass Band led a procession of children, all carrying flowers, round the centre of the town.

Just one year later the door of a fine new Congregational Church was unlocked. Members of the church, carrying banners, took part in another procession.

From that time on, out of school hours, their Chapel School was only used for social and money-raising events. As social occasions, TEA PARTIES were still very popular, and the bright ladies of the WOMEN'S FELLOWSHIP thought up original and intriguing ideas to attract people to their special meals such as:

- PINK TEAS: men serving *[in pink pinnies?]*

- FLOWER GIRL TEAS.

- GYPSY TEAS with a fortune teller present.

After the teas, amusing competitions were held such as "Nail-driving into wood" for ladies and "Hat-trimming" for men. *[What excitement!]*

CHRIST CHURCH

The Vicarage, North Road, now overlooks the Welmar Estate. The path over the bridge leads to the High School

The second vicar of the parish, the Reverend Scott, started a building fund in 1897 to pay for proposed extensions to the church and for the building of a vicarage in Upper North Road. When erected, this fine house stood alone with magnificent, uninterrupted views over the canal below, across to Kellet Seeds (a tree-covered hill) and the hills of the Pennine Chain.

[The building now overlooks the Welmar Estate.]

THE PARISH CHURCH MISSION HALL

Churches provided the biggest part of Carnforth's social life. In 1898, Christ Church built a PARISH HALL (popularly known as THE CHURCH ROOM) in PRESTON STREET, which became the venue for a wide variety of events, such as Tea Parties, Concerts, Bazaars, Sales of Work, Conversaziones etc. (The dictionary's description of the latter is a soirée given by a learned or art society. Well, well!)

A WHITE SALE was typical of the times. Many articles in everyday use were always WHITE: towels, table-linen, bed-linen, underwear, nightwear (NOT including pyjamas for men. Carnforth chaps had not got around to those yet), duchess-sets, antimacassars, handkerchiefs, d'oyleys etc.

[Pity the work-weary women having to deal with such a wash when laundry equipment consisted of dolly-tubs, dolly-legs, mangles and flat irons!]

THE ROMAN CATHOLICS

There was no place of worship for people of the Roman Catholic faith in Carnforth - no church, no school, no church hall.

Those strong in their faith walked to St Mary of the Angels Church in Bolton-le Sands. Their children attended school in Carnforth until they were 7 years old, and then made the long, daily trek to the R.C. School at Bolton-le-Sands, come hail, rain or snow, carrying their dinners in neat newspaper-wrapped packages.

OUR OLD QUEEN - GOD BLESS HER AGAIN!

In 1897, Children were again presented with commemorative mugs as souvenirs, this time for Queen Victoria's Diamond Jubilee - sixty glorious years as our sovereign. The town celebrated the auspicious occasion with waving flags, patriotic tunes, red-white-and-blue bunting, processions and an enjoyable Field Day.

A NAUGHTY CITIZEN

JOHN SMITH, ex-policeman, ex-coal-dealer, ex-fire-brigade man (and ex-GOOD CARNFORTHIAN!) was summonsed for THREATENING to kill his wife and daughter.

MORE PUBLICITY

Mr W J WEEKS, sole proprietor of the CARNFORTH AND DISTRICT BILL-POSTING COMPANY, printed handbills at 1s 6d per 1,000 as a means of advertising.

"Advertising is to business what steam is to machinery: the propelling power!" he said in the CARNFORTH REMINDER, which delivered 2,000 copies monthly.

A town crier would have been an asset!

Large bills, posted on several wooden hoardings around the town, and on the gable-ends of houses, were another form of advertising.

THE IRON WORKS

The production of steel at the Iron Works had never been very successful and, by 1899, it had closed down completely.

(Iron continued to be produced sporadically for another 24 years.)

THE END OF THE 19th CENTURY

Carnforth's population had increased tenfold in 50 years: in 1851 it numbered 294 and in 1901 it had grown to 3,040.

During those busy, bustling years, Carnforth had changed from a quiet hamlet to an important little town.

Workers from different cultures had settled here from Cumberland, Westmorland, Yorkshire, Cheshire and the Midlands. In spite of a wide variety of dialects, they managed to understand each other after a while, but differences did exist. Some parents were known as PA and MA, others as MUTHER and FATHER (to rhyme with GATHER) or as T'OWD LASS AND T'OWD FELLA.

Pronunciations differed e.g.:

    1) THERE could be thur or thee-er.

    2) WHERE was wur or wee-er etc.

Radio and TV were away in the future, so standardised English had not arrived. Down at the Iron Works and on the railway, some of the following questions and remarks might have been heard (hurd, hee-ard):

"Wot's thou doo-ing, laking ovver thee-er?"

"Wee-er wur thee last neet?"

"Wur dust think thou's gangin'?"

"Ow ister Jim?" "I's nobbut middlin."

"Aster sin yon lass fray Cragbank?" "She's a reet corker!"

"Duster wanna goo ooam?"

"Canter cum tut pub wi mi?"

"Sister, at you lazy slonk!"

"Shurrup an' gerr on wi' thy dikin."

"Eigh, wot dust think about yon couple next doo-er?" "She's a reet funny ossity an' he's a rum joker I'll tell thee!"

A YOUNG CARNFORTHIAN'S COURTING PROGRAMME:

    1) Clickin' wi' a lass.

    2) Knockin 'er off.

    3) 'Angin' 'is 'at up.

    4) Gerrin' 'is feet under t'table.

    5) Gerrin' wed.

LOCAL WORDS CAME INTO COMMON USAGE

The prizes for card and board games were often:

    1) "T'rabbuts on Kellet Seeds" (an eminence which has since been carried away on lorries

in the form of limestone rocks).

2) Unwanted questions about where one had been could get the answer: "Up suff at t'back of Hartley's." (Someone had gone wrong somewhere a suff was a sort of drain.)

3) A K-EYE-CLE (local pronunciation) was a jacket made of denim-like material. It was issued to most railwaymen as part of their uniform. (Was this word derived from the old word KIRTLE a man's tunic or coat?)

TO SUMMARISE

The establishment of the IRON WORKS in 1864 had been the first factor in the town's development. Sadly they were not now flourishing and the production of steel had ended. It was disappointing that the impetus they had gained originally, by having a good supply of local, phosphorus-free haematite iron-ore, had not been maintained for long. When other iron works learnt how to overcome the problem of phosphorus in their ores, Carnforth found that it had many strong rivals, and its trade went into recession.

The second factor in the town's progress was the growth of THE RAILWAYS, which had made it into a busy junction. The canal was now owned by the railway companies, and barges drawn by horses were still useful for the transportation of heavy and bulky loads. The canal also supplied the railway with water. (The opening of an underground pipeline to the railway-sheds can still be seen under the bank of the canal basin.)

The continued demand for sand and gravel, used in the building of roads etc., meant that local pits were kept very busy.

As the population continued to grow, more and more shops opened and the number of MEN employed in the retail trade increased.

Carnforth's churches and chapels were well established by the year 1900, and were full of ardent worshippers. They provided a full and interesting SOCIAL LIFE for their followers.

INTO THE 20th CENTURY

As Carnforth went forward into the new century, wheels were helping its inhabitants to travel further afield. The whole of Great Britain was opening up for them, especially for those employed by the railway, which gave them the advantage of cheap and even free travel. The 'Iron Horse' was still well ahead in the field of locomotion, but 4-wheeled, horseless carriages had just entered the race. The day of the car was not very far distant. So what had the future in store for Carnforth? The possibility of it growing to the size of Barrow seemed unlikely but, as a developing railway town, the outlook was bright. Several questions were still to be answered:

Would the Iron Works eventually close down and cause serious unemployment?

Would new work come into the town?

This tale is continued in the next book in the series: ***How Carnforth Steamed into the 20th Century***.

THE GROWTH OF THE POPULATION

YEAR	NUMBER OF INHABITANTS	
1801	219 (Bolton-le-Sands had 639)	
1821	294	
1841	299	
1851	294	
1861	393 (The coming of the Iron Works 1864)	
1871	1,091	THE
1881	2,000 approx.	GROWTH
1901	3,040	OF
1911	3,142	THE
1921	3,247	RAILWAYS

REFERENCES

JOHN LUCAS'S HISTORY OF WARTON PARISH
(by courtesy of Mrs M Gregson)
Edited by John Rowlinson Ford and J Fuller-
Maitland, in 1931.
Printers: Titus Wilson & Son. Kendal.

THE MEMORANDUM OF JAMES ERVING
Recorded by Anne Hyelman in Lancashire Life.

TOPOGRAPHY & DIRECTORY OF LANCASTER AND
16 MILES AROUND
by P Mannex.

BULMER'S DIRECTORIES (several annual editions).

THE BUILDING OF THE LANCASTER CANAL
by Robert Philpots.

FAST PACKET BOATS ON THE LANCASTER CANAL
by Andrew White.

LOOKING AT HISTORY
by R J Unstead.

VICTORIAN LOCAL HISTORY VOLUME 8
Morecambe Library.

CARNFORTH IN VICTORIAN TIMES
Lancaster Reference Library.

SHORT HISTORY OF CHRIST CHURCH
by courtesy of Ian Pearson.

GUIDE TO CARNFORTH & DISTRICT
Published in 1908.
Printed by Weeks, Market Street, Carnforth.

CARNFORTH BROCHURE
Published in London circa 1921.

WARTON IN THE MIDDLE AGES
by P H W Booth.

THE CENSUS FORM OF 1871, 1881 & 1891
(Viewed at Lancaster University & Lancaster
Reference Library).

Many extracts from THE GAZETTE, CARNFORTH
WEEKLY NEWS, CARNFORTH'S MONTHLY
REMINDER
By courtesy of the present editor, various
references to old copies of THE LANCASTER
GUARDIAN.

TURNPIKES & TOLL HOUSES OF LANCASHIRE
by Ron Freethy.

CENTENARY OF THE EMMANUEL CONGREGATION
CHURCH
by courtesy of Mrs Ruth Badley.

If you have enjoyed this book, please consider reviewing it on Amazon or Goodreads (or both).

And feel free visit the Lundarien Press website for more titles by Marion Russell and other authors:

www.lundarienpress.com